© Copyright 2024 David Merritt (Uncle Dave) All rights reserved. No part of this publication may be reproduced, distributed, or transmitted in any form or by any means, including photocopying, recording, or other electronic or mechanical methods, without the prior written permission of the author except in the case of brief quotations embodied in critical reviews and certain other noncommercial uses permitted by copyright law. For permission requests, contact dreamsinspiregreatness@gmail.com.

Special Thanks:
Thank you to all who have supported me through this journey. A special thanks goes to my best friend. Thank you for being a great example for me. Thank you for continuing to motivate me!

The MotivAte B, C's

You're AWESOME! You absolutely are my friend.

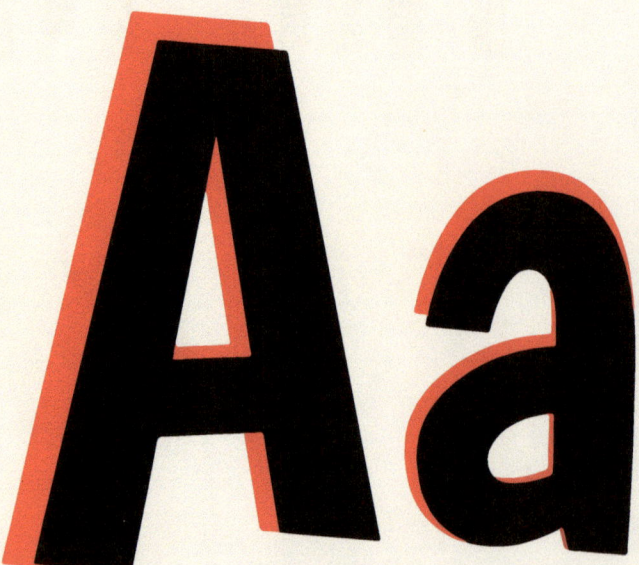

Staying CALM is the best time to clearly think and see.

Cc

Design who you DREAM to be.

Ff

Hold on to your **FAITH**.
Keep your beliefs in sight.

Continue to GROW and get better.
It's ok to make mistakes.

Hold on to **HOPE**, no matter how long it takes.

Use your IMAGINATION! Just think of what you could be.

OPPORTUNITY is all around you. Look and see!

PREPARE for the possibilities.

QUALITY work is what you should aim to do.

Enjoy your REWARDS, after your work is through.

Be TEACHABLE so the learning never ends.

You are UNIQUE. One of a kind. There's no one like you.

The WORLD is a WONDEROUS place. Prepare for an awesome ride.

Let's see the world

World! Here we come!

Create an extraordinary and XENIAL life. Live life and thrive.

Stay YOUNG AT HEART. Keep moving! Don't stand still.

About the Author:
Thank you for coming along with me on this adventure. I've spent years reading about leadership and growing myself. After working with students for many years, I thought about being able to share leadership principles in a story format during a child's foundational years. It's my belief that when someone decides to build their dreams, what's most important in the beginning is building their foundation first. It's our foundations that our dreams are built and stand on. It's my hope that my books will be an effective tool and assist in laying down the foundation for people to grow and build their dreams. Thank you!

www.ingramcontent.com/pod-product-compliance
Lightning Source LLC
Chambersburg PA
CBHW060759090426
42736CB00002B/93